Saint Damien of Molokai

Saint Damien of Molokai
Hero of Hawaii

Written by Virginia Helen Richards, FSP,
and D. Thomas Halpin, FSP

Illustrated by Anne Bergstrom

Pauline
BOOKS & MEDIA
Boston

Library of Congress Cataloging-in-Publication Data

Richards, Virginia Helen.
  Saint Damien of Molokai : hero of Hawaii / written by Virginia
Helen Richards and D. Thomas Halpin ; illustrated by Anne
Bergstrom.
    p. cm. — (Encounter the saints series ; 25)
    ISBN 0-8198-7126-5 (pbk.)
  1. Damien, Father, 1840-1889. 2. Catholic Church—Hawaii—
Clergy—Biography. 3. Missionaries—Hawaii—Biography. 4.
Missionaries—Belgium—Biography. 5. Missions to leprosy
patients—Hawaii. I. Halpin, Deborah Thomas. II. Title.
  BX4705.D25R53 2009
  266'.2092—dc22
  [B]
                                    2009013784

"P" and PAULINE are registered trademarks of the Daughters of
St. Paul.

Copyright © 2009, Daughters of St. Paul

Published by Pauline Books & Media, 50 Saint Pauls Avenue,
Boston, MA 02130-3491

Printed in the U.S.A.

www.pauline.org

Pauline Books & Media is the publishing house of the
Daughters of St. Paul, an international congregation of women
religious serving the Church with the communications media.

1 2 3 4 5 6 7 8 9   13 12 11 10 09

Encounter the Saints Series

Saint Francis of Assisi
Gentle Revolutionary

Saint Ignatius of Loyola
For the Greater Glory of God

Saint Isaac Jogues
With Burning Heart

Saint Joan of Arc
God's Soldier

Saint John Vianney
A Priest for All People

Saint Juan Diego
And Our Lady of Guadalupe

Saint Katharine Drexel
The Total Gift

Saint Martin de Porres
Humble Healer

Saint Maximilian Kolbe
Mary's Knight

Saint Paul
The Thirteenth Apostle

Saint Pio of Pietrelcina
Rich in Love

Saint Teresa of Avila
Joyful in the Lord

Saint Thérèse of Lisieux
The Way of Love

For other children's titles on the saints, visit our Web
site: www.pauline.org.

CONTENTS

1

A Close Call

The old bell clanged loudly, cutting through the quiet afternoon air. In Tremelo, Belgium, school was over. The students scattered quickly, heading for home. The De Veuster brothers and sisters and a group of their friends pushed and shoved, chatting as they walked along.

"Hey! Let's play crack the whip!" one of the girls called out.

"I'm not sure that's such a good idea. Sometimes people drive their carts down this road," cautioned ten-year-old Auguste. The younger children hesitated a moment.

"Oh, we'll be careful! Come on, it will be fun!" said Joseph. He was just three years younger than his brother Auguste. Joseph grabbed Auguste's hand and started running. The others quickly followed suit, joining hands along the empty country road. The object of the game was simply to run as fast as you could and not lose your grip. It was a challenge to stay balanced and to keep up with the faster runners in the group.

"Hang on tight! I see a curve ahead!" Joseph shouted. They tightened their grip on each other and swung around the arc. This was the fun part!

But suddenly they heard the sound of hoofbeats ahead—four huge horses and a noisy wooden cart were about to round the bend from the opposite direction. The driver panicked when he saw the children in the street and pulled back with all his might on the reins to halt his team. Screaming filled the air as the children ran to get out of the way of the horses. Then there was silence ...

The cart rumbled to a stop several yards down the road. The driver, with his heart thundering in his ears, leaped off his seat and ran back to the bend in the road, searching frantically for the children. One by one, they were climbing out of a shallow ditch on the roadside, where they had jumped to avoid his cart. *Thank goodness!* thought the driver, wiping the sweat from his forehead. *No one is hurt.*

"What were you children doing? Don't ever take a risk like that again!" the driver scolded.

But Auguste wasn't listening. "Where is Joseph?" he asked as he stood on the road again.

The driver's heart jumped to his throat. Had someone been injured after all?

"That sure was close!" a familiar voice called out from the opposite side of the road. The driver squinted and realized that a little boy—perhaps seven or eight years old—was speaking. It was Joseph.

"Are you all right?" the driver asked, running to him.

Joseph De Veuster stood up and brushed the dirt off his pants. "Oh, I'm fine," he said. "I was just thanking my guardian angel for watching out for us." Then, turning to Auguste, he added, "I told you we'd be careful!"

The De Veuster family lived in the northern region of Belgium known as Flanders. The people of Flanders, often referred to as Flemings, spoke Dutch and farmed the flat land of their region. Joseph's father, Francis De Veuster, grew and sold grain. It was a good living, and the large family was well provided for.

After the children finally returned home that evening, the family crowded together in their large farmhouse kitchen for the evening meal. Catherine De Veuster turned from her place at the fireplace where she had been stirring the thick Flemish soup for supper. She gazed for a moment on the healthy young faces of her children: Auguste, Leonce, Gerard, Eugenie, Pauline, Marie, Constance ... and Joseph. He was her second youngest child and had been born January 3, 1840. What a knack he had for getting into mischief! She had already heard about his latest escapade.

But then Catherine smiled, almost in spite of herself. *God has certainly blessed our family,* she thought. *We have to work very hard sometimes, but we're happy!*

"Tonight *I* get to sit by Mama!" Marie announced, breaking into her mother's reverie.

"You *always* get to sit by her! It's not fair!" the others complained.

"Not *all* the time," she said, tossing her head back in defense.

Suddenly the tall figure of a man appeared in the doorway.

"Are those my children I hear arguing?" Papa De Veuster feigned astonishment. Silence filled the dining room.

Joseph shook his head solemnly and answered mischievously, "Not *us*, Papa."

"Joseph!" His father's gaze fell on him in concern. "What happened to your head? Where did that lump come from? It looks like a mountain!" He reached his hand out to Joseph. "Let me take a look at you."

Sheepishly, Joseph came forward, his large, dark eyes fixed on his father. Sure enough, there it was, a big lump on his forehead that even his curly hair couldn't hide.

"You weren't trying to scare Farmer Jan's horses again, were you, Joseph?"

"No, Papa, of course not. I remember what you said last time. We were only playing a game!" Joseph replied.

Mama's voice trembled a little as she explained, "It was a bit of a miracle. We must thank the good God that none of the children were seriously hurt today, Papa." Then she recounted the misadventure.

Papa sighed and surveyed his children. "I trust that in the future you'll keep your games *off the road?*" Eight heads nodded energetically. "All right then, I won't say another word about it. But the next time I hear you've been playing crack the whip, it had better be in an open field where it's safe!"

2

GROWING UP IN BELGIUM

Joseph's close call on the road home from school wasn't his first—or his last—childhood adventure. He loved excitement, and in the winter, when the Dyle River was frozen over, Joseph joined his friends in skating races. The competition could be fierce!

"Joseph, faster! Gerard is right behind you!" the crowd of onlookers shouted excitedly.

Joseph's blood pulsed with excitement. He bit his lip and pumped faster and faster, flying forward in a burst of speed. The children cheered. Joseph had passed the finish line. But with the wind on his face, the exhilarating sensation of being on air, and the trees whizzing by in a blur of light and shadows, he was having too much fun to stop now!

A few of the children looked at one another in concern. "The ice is too thin out there. We never go out that far ... what's he thinking?"

"Joseph, stop! Come back!" they shouted with their hands cupped around their mouths. "Come back!"

But he was too far away to hear them. And the cold air felt so good.

Then, in a flash, he noticed the thin ice ahead—cracks had begun to form and water was seeping onto the ice. "I can't stop!" The words caught in his throat. "I'm heading straight for it!" Horrible chills went up his spine as he heard the ice cracking under him.

With one huge effort he cut his glide and pushed with every muscle of his body into a sideways swerve, narrowly avoiding the dangerous area. As he slowed, Joseph thought again of his guardian angel, who always had a new reason to watch out for him. It seemed that he kept his angel working double time.

When Joseph and his brothers and sisters managed to stay out of trouble, Mama often made time for a special treat. At the end of a long day, she would reach for a big book that sat on the shelf over the fireplace. The children loved to listen to her read from it. She would wipe her hands carefully on her apron and then sit down in her wicker rocking chair with the younger children gathered around her.

The ancient brown book was full of exciting pictures and stories of saints, hermits, and martyrs. They were people who helped those in need; they fasted, prayed, and did great things for God. Mama would read slowly, with emphasis, and the children would listen, their imaginations taking off. These saints were their heroes and heroines, and the children dreamed of being like them.

One day after school, Joseph called a few of his brothers and sisters together. "Listen," he said, "I've got an idea!" Joseph might have been one of the youngest of the group, but his ideas were *always* good! "I've been thinking about those stories Mama reads to us. Why don't we do what the hermits did?"

The vote was unanimous. It would be an adventure—they would be just like the saints who stayed out in the desert, living in silence, growing in friendship with God. They'd be saints in no time! There certainly weren't any deserts in Belgium, but then Auguste remembered a quiet clearing in the forest behind the schoolhouse. No one would bother them there. Each of the children staked out a spot for a "hermitage." Everything went quiet as they began their serious work of imitating the prayerful hermits. After a while, it was hard to stay so silent and to keep on praying. But the children were determined to stick it out—for a couple of hours, at least.

Soon darkness set in, but neither Joseph nor the others had any idea that a frantic search was being made for them. Their worried parents finally found the would-be hermits in the forest clearing. By this time, the children were wishing they were home eating supper, but no one wanted to be the first to call off the attempt at a life of prayer and penance …

"Here they are, Papa! Behind the schoolhouse—I've found them!" Mama called in relief. Papa strode into the clearing.

"Whose great idea was this?" he demanded, searching for the ringleader. Joseph inched his way forward. "Would you like to tell me what is going on here?" asked Papa, a bit more calmly.

"Well, um, we like the stories Mama reads to us from that old book, Papa," Joseph explained simply. "We decided that we would be saintly hermits too!"

Papa turned and looked at Mama, who tried to keep a straight face. Taking her husband by the arm, she said, "Papa, let's go home. I'll explain it later if I can."

Through the dark night the family trudged home. As they neared the red brick farmhouse with the welcome light of its windows, Papa gathered the family together. "You know, one of the ways the saints became saints was by being obedient. From now on, you're to be home by dark. And tomorrow you're to come straight home from school and help me with the farm chores. Understood?" he said. Then with a smile he added, "Now let's get inside. Mama's lovely supper has been waiting a long time for you."

Joseph and his siblings exchanged surprised looks. It looked as though they were getting off easy this time. Without another word, they raced inside. Being a hermit—even for an afternoon—was hard work, and they were hungry!

3

Dreams for the Future

Joseph may have only been playing at being saints with his siblings, but his family's faith made a deep impression on him as a child. Mornings and evenings, his family prayed together. In this way, Joseph began to develop his own friendship with God—a friendship that grew stronger as Joseph grew up.

On Palm Sunday, 1850, Joseph made his first Communion. He was ten years old. (In those days first Communion was received at an older age.) Besides his knack for getting into mischief, Joseph also displayed a generous heart and was sensitive to others' needs.

One warm summer's morning, Mama De Veuster baked her delicious *speculoos*—Flemish spice cookies. She filled a little bag with the cookies, fresh from the oven and still warm, and handed it to Leonce as he, Joseph, and Pauline set off for a walk. They had finished their morning chores and were looking forward to a few hours of freedom in the bright sun. They hadn't gone far when the tantalizing aroma wafting from the cookies began to make their stomachs growl.

"Leonce, let's stop here and try Mama's cookies," Pauline suggested. Joseph and Leonce were only too willing to give in.

They were just dividing the cookies among themselves when they noticed a little boy had approached and was watching them. His clothing was threadbare and he had no shoes.

"Could I have a cookie too?" he asked shyly.

Mouths remained open and cookies paused in midair. The children looked at each other and hesitated. *He does look hungry,* they thought. *I suppose we could share one with him …*

But Joseph was quicker than the others "Sure, you can have *all* the cookies," he said, scooping them up and handing them to the boy—as Leonce and Pauline stared in disbelief. But that was Joseph's kind heart.

By the time Joseph was thirteen, he had completed his studies at the town school. It had taught him all that it could offer. Joseph stayed home for the next four years to help on the farm, along with Leonce and Gerard.

They were four long years filled with hard work. Early every morning he rose with the sun to begin his duties. He cared for the animals and spent steady hours under the hot sun, working the soil, cultivating, planting, and harvesting. Plowing was hard work, but Joseph held his own. At night he'd collapse on his bed, weary and aching, but happy to have helped the family.

One day, Joseph was working in the fields with his older brother Leonce. "Hey, Joseph! Over here! Toss that one if you can!" teased Leonce.

"What do you mean, *if I can?*" laughed Joseph. Into the air the bale of hay flew, like an autumn leaf caught in the wind.

"Watch out!" shouted Leonce, jumping clear of the bale.

"You asked for it!" shot back Joseph, grinning widely.

His father watched with pride as Joseph heaved the golden bales of hay high above his head as if they were pillows. The villagers of Tremelo envied such strength. Plans grew in his father's mind. This fine son of his would make a good companion in the grain business. Francis De Veuster had seen his son at work and realized that not only was he strong, but he was also intelligent.

On May 15, 1858, at the age of eighteen, Joseph resumed his studies, this time travel-

Francis watched with pride as Joseph worked on the farm. This fine son would make a good companion in the grain business.

ing to Braine-le-Comte, a college of commercial business in the French-speaking southern region of Belgium. There he was to learn French in order to fulfill his father's dreams, for businessmen in Belgium had to speak both Dutch and French. It was difficult at first to get used to studying again. Accustomed to fresh farm air, Joseph felt cooped up in the study halls. He yearned to feel the good earth in his hands again, and as time passed he noticed, with a twinge of sadness, that the hard-won calluses on his strong hands were growing softer.

He hadn't lost his love of study, however. He attacked this new occupation as he had the challenge of farming: with the same patient, plodding effort. And the teachers and his fellow students grew to love and admire the husky young Fleming who was always so quick with a smile.

Meanwhile, back home in Tremelo, Papa De Veuster read his son's letters with a pride that was growing by leaps and bounds. His dreams for Joseph were alive with hopes of huge success. Papa had no idea of the things happening deep within young Joseph's soul … things known only between Joseph and God!

4

LETTERS

It was late. Everyone in the school dormitory was fast asleep. Even those who always stayed awake as late as possible to study had put out their lamps long before. The shuffling steps of the director making his midnight rounds suddenly halted in the corridor. What was that light up ahead? It was coming from Joseph's room! He scratched his chin. *Hmmm …* the director thought. *There aren't any exams tomorrow, at least not in Joseph's class. But then this isn't the first time I've noticed his light so late …*

The kindly director was determined to find out what was going on. Silently and slowly, he opened the door just a crack. There in the corner the young student knelt before a crucifix, lost in prayer. *What kind of teenager would be praying so intently in the middle of the night?* the director thought. *Sure, Joseph is a good student, but I had no idea this side of his life existed. I guess only God judges the heart.* In respectful silence the man closed the door again.

Since his arrival in Braine-le-Comte, Joseph had begun thinking seriously about his future. It had seemed so natural to begin working in the family business, but now Joseph was having second thoughts. His heart was being pulled in another direction. But how could he ever tell his father what he really wanted to do?

Then July came and, with it, the news that his sister Pauline, who had entered a convent, had made her religious profession. She was now a religious sister, totally dedicated to God. Joseph was deeply impressed by this. This seemed like the moment to reveal to his parents what had been on his mind. So he wrote a letter home. It came as quite a surprise to his unsuspecting father.

"How happy Pauline must be!" Joseph wrote. "She has taken on quite a challenge. *My turn* will come soon, I hope. Wouldn't it be wonderful if I could join my brother Pamphile at the seminary?"

Joseph's brother Auguste had begun to study for the priesthood and had joined a religious community dedicated to the Sacred Hearts of Jesus and Mary. Auguste had taken a new name—Pamphile—to show that his life was now completed dedicated to God.

Joseph's letter hit the red brick house at Tremelo like a boulder!

"Now, calm down, Francis," Mama De Veuster soothed.

"Calm down? Catherine, how can I be calm? He never mentioned this to me before! I thought he wanted to work in the family business. Who will help me if Joseph really leaves?" With Joseph's crumpled letter in his hand he restlessly paced the floor. "After all the sacrifices I've made! He has a prosperous career cut out for him! What is he thinking?"

Mama De Veuster understood. Papa *had* made sacrifices for Joseph's education— sacrifices that had streaked his hair with grey. School tuition didn't come out of the clouds. It had cost Papa hard-earned savings and long days of work.

"Maybe," Papa De Veuster said, settling down as he reasoned, "maybe it's just an idea, a passing phase. I've already given enough of my children to God. Joseph *can't* go. I'm counting on him."

Letters went back and forth between father and son. But Joseph didn't show any signs of changing his mind. Soon October came and the leaves changed, painting the landscape with beautiful hues of golden yellow, orange, and fiery red. It was announced that there would be a parish mission in Braine-le-Comte—days of special prayer, preaching, and opportunities to go to Mass and Confession. This was an especially grace-filled time for the people of the parish, and Joseph went, eager to find strength in his search for a way to do God's will. Joseph thought that God was calling him to serve as a religious, but his father refused to accept this possibility. Francis's disappointment with his son tore at Joseph's heart.

But during the parish mission, the call of God renewed itself even more intensely. Joseph continued his nightly vigils of prayer, pouring out his struggles to the Lord. "I love my family, Lord," he prayed with his head bowed low, "but I love you even more. Help my father understand. Show me how I can follow your call, no matter the cost."

Soon after, his brother Pamphile was sent by his religious community to the Belgian city of Louvain. He invited Joseph to come and visit him in December.

"No matter what father says, Joseph, this is your decision," Pamphile reminded his brother firmly.

Joseph swallowed hard. "I know, I know," he said. "I hate to disappoint him. But now that you have introduced me to your own religious community, I feel strongly that this is where God wants me."

"Then go ahead," Pamphile nodded. "Don't be afraid. The Lord will see you through as he did for me."

Joseph returned to the college at Braine-le-Comte, and on Christmas Day he began to write—one final plea, hoping that his father would understand. Outside, lazy snowflakes drifted to the ground. Strains of Christmas carols could be heard from just outside the windows.

"Father and Mother, I wanted so much to write to you today, on this beautiful feast of Christmas. I am convinced, now more than ever, that God is calling me to dedicate my life completely to his service. I know that this disappoints you, but I hope that you can understand. If God calls me, I must obey."

Papa De Veuster held the letter in his shaking hands as he read it aloud to Mama. In silence as deep as the winter night around the De Veuster home, Papa stood still, head bent. Mama saw a tear in his eye and leaned against him. Turning his head,

20

Papa whispered, "I hope he is doing the right thing, Catherine. I will miss him ..."

Mama hugged her husband. "We'll pray for him, Francis. Everything will be all right." Snow fell silently as they stared out into the night, hoping Joseph knew what he was doing.

And so, at the beginning of the new year in 1859, Francis De Veuster made a surprise visit to Joseph in Braine-le-Comte. He accompanied his son to the monastery in Louvain, where Father Vincke, the superior, accepted Joseph into the community. Francis returned to his farm in Tremelo alone. Catherine was waiting for him. For some time now, they had had a feeling it would end this way. Sometimes parents just know these things.

5

CALL ME "BROTHER DAMIEN"

The Congregation of the Sacred Hearts of Jesus and Mary had been founded by Father Pierre Coudrin in 1800. Father Coudrin envisioned a community of priests and brothers who would be dedicated to a special mission: traveling all over the world to teach people about the love of Jesus and Mary. They would also be devoted to continual adoration of Jesus in the Eucharist. This was *just* what Joseph wanted.

He focused himself on his new way of life with all his heart and soul. There were many new things to learn, tasks to do, rules to get accustomed to. But Joseph attacked each challenge with boundless energy. And a new challenge was about to present itself!

Although Joseph had loved his studies, his knowledge of French would not help him on the road to the priesthood. In order to celebrate Mass at the time, priests needed to know Latin. Most of the other young men in the monastery had already mastered the language. But nineteen-year-old Joseph hadn't even begun. It was suggested that perhaps he should set his sights on becoming a religious brother and not a priest.

With a heavy heart, young Joseph knelt before Jesus in the tabernacle. Joseph tried to fix his gaze on his God present in the small white host. *It's true,* he thought, *I don't know Latin. And I'm most at home on a farm. I'm really at a disadvantage.*

Joseph wasn't about to give up entirely, however. He bowed his head and prayed, "If it's your will, Lord, help me to overcome these obstacles. You can do *everything!* I believe this with all my heart!"

In February Joseph received the religious habit, the distinctive white cassock that all the members of his community wore, and took the name "Damien." He was now a novice, a student in his religious community, preparing to take his vows as a brother. Damien had not given up his dream of the priesthood, though. Learning Latin would take a lot of prayer, determination, and constant practice. Fortunately, Pamphile helped Damien whenever they were able to get together during the day.

During the next six months, Damien studied with determination. Pamphile was thrilled with his brother's tremendous progress and reported it to the superior. It was finally decided that Damien *would* go on to study for the priesthood! He would enter Father Verhaege's class of novices studying for ordination. Damien's dream would come true!

One day during a class lecture, Father Verhaege's voice cut into Damien's intense thought. "Brother Damien, what are you doing?" Slowly, the other students turned in their desks to see Damien's penknife hovering over his desk. Deep in concentration, Damien hadn't realized that he was carving his notes right onto the surface of his wooden desk!

Damien turned red and put the penknife down.

Father Verhaege straightened his spectacles as he came down the aisle. "Do you know," he asked, "that defacing the property of the Congregation is against the vow of poverty?" The novice master peered over his glasses to read what Brother Damien had carved into his desk: *prayer* and *penance*.

"From now on," Father Verhaege advised, "it will be better if you carve these words on your heart." Shaking his head, he turned away, barely concealing a smile.

Brother Damien was no ready-made saint, far from it. In some ways, he was still the boy Joseph De Veuster, with a knack for getting into trouble. But Father Verhaege would later say that in all his years of experience he had never met a more lovable or sociable young man than Brother Damien.

6

AN UNEXPECTED CALL

Damien professed his vows on October 7, 1860, when he was just twenty years old. He then moved to Paris to study Greek, Latin, and philosophy at the headquarters of the Congregation of the Sacred Hearts of Jesus and Mary.

Once again he dived into his assignment with boundless energy. Often he stayed up far into the evening to study. "I have so much to catch up on," he would explain to friends who urged him to lighten up.

But that was not the only reason he pushed so hard. Damien's heart was once again full of big dreams. Damien wanted to be an apostle and join his religious brothers who were lucky enough to be sent to distant mission lands.

One night, a visiting missionary bishop from the Pacific islands spoke to the community of the needs in his distant terri-tory. Damien's heart was on fire after that. He wrote letter after letter to Pamphile, each brimming with excitement. "Christ died to save all people. But how many people still have never even heard of Jesus? Wouldn't it be great if you and I could join the ranks of our missionary brothers?" Pamphile wholeheartedly agreed.

The young brother studied even harder, looking to the future in which he hoped he would be an apostle of Christ. Day by day, he continued to pore over his books, leaving little time for rest. Although Damien was physically strong, the long hours of strain and the poor lighting in his little room took a heavy toll on his eyes. By that summer Damien was already wearing the thick, wire-rimmed glasses that would be his for the rest of his life.

Autumn came once again, and Damien returned to Louvain in Belgium to continue his studies in theology and philosophy. Happily, he found himself sharing a room with his brother. It was great to be together again. Sometimes they remembered the funny things that had happened back home in Tremelo. They also spoke of the struggles they shared as followers of Christ. Damien enjoyed the year as a gift from God, and both brothers would remember it for the rest of their lives.

Finally, in 1863, the great day of ordina-tion came for Pamphile. Damien was almost as excited as his brother! And when Pamphile celebrated his first Mass, the entire De Veuster family was reunited for the memorable event. Soon after it was announced that six Sacred Hearts priests and brothers had been chosen to go to the Hawaiian Islands (which were also known as the Sandwich Islands at that time), where the bishop was pleading for their help. To the surprise of Damien, Father Pamphile was among those chosen. And on top of that, they would be leaving very soon. Damien wondered and prayed ... Would he ever get his turn? Was it God's will that he be a missionary, too? Then a tragedy occurred.

Before the missionary priests ever left their homeland, typhoid fever swept over Louvain like a blanket of death. Every home had its victims. Terror struck the hearts of all, including the students and staff of the seminary.

At the time, there was no cure for the disease. Those who were not bedridden had to care for those who were. One night, Father Pamphile stumbled into the room. His mind was a dizzy haze. He clung to the table, then the chair, finally collapsing on the bed. Damien dropped his books with a crash and scrambled over the suitcase and trunk that were already packed for his brother's voyage.

"No, it can't be," Damien whispered to himself. His brother had contracted the dreaded fever!

Day and night Damien took care of Pamphile, keeping a worried vigil at his bedside. "You've got to get well," he said anxiously.

Father Pamphile nodded weakly. He did get better slowly, but it was evident that he would need months to fully recover. He was one of the lucky ones who survived the deadly disease.

What now? Damien thought hard and prayed. A missionary was needed to take Father Pamphile's place. It was true that Damien wasn't a priest yet, but he thought there might be work for him as a helper to the other priests. What was stopping him from volunteering? He took his plan to his brother, and they worked out a few details. There wasn't a moment to lose, so Damien wrote a letter to the superior general, the priest who served and governed the Sacred Hearts priests and brothers throughout the world. It was a step that took courage and faith, but time would show that Damien possessed abundant reserves of both. In no time, his letter was on its way to Paris. Waiting for a reply would be a test of patience.

At breakfast one morning, the answer came. Father Superior approached the table where Damien was eating. Suddenly the clanging of dishware and the noise of conversation died down to a respectful silence. Damien looked up from his plate into the stern face that stared down at him. Father Superior gave him the letter, saying, "Brother Damien, it was rather hasty of you to want this before your ordination. But, very well. You *are* to go to the islands."

Damien felt his heart leap for joy. It was the answer he was waiting for, the letter that would change his life forever. He hardly noticed the surprised reactions of his companions. Nothing else mattered at the moment but that his dream had come true!

7

"LEAVE YOUR COUNTRY"

Damien looked out over the vast expanse of water stretching endlessly away. The narrow strip of land he was leaving disappeared on the horizon. His heart ached, he had to admit, but he told himself that this must be what Abraham had experienced when he left his homeland. The example of the Old Testament hero gave him courage.

"Leave your country," God had told Abraham, "and go to a new land. I will lead you." Damien also remembered that many of the first followers of Christ were called to leave their homes and their loved ones, too. He was in good company.

Damien stared into the sparkling blue water, still thinking about the farewell visit to his family. But it was remembering the look on Papa De Veuster's face that made him ache the most.

"A missionary? You, my son?" Papa De Veuster asked in a choked voice. "Then I shall never see you again?" Their eyes met, and it was Damien who broke the gaze. He was usually so ready with an answer. But not now. The silence between them was painful.

The next morning he met his mother at the shrine of Our Lady of Montaigu for one last farewell. Damien loved this shrine and had wanted one last look before he left home. His mother held his hand as she did when he was little. Together they knelt before the miraculous statue of Mary, praying for each other.

"I asked the Queen of all the Apostles to bless you, my son," the small woman told him. "I won't be able to take care of you anymore." He read in her eyes the words she wanted to say but couldn't bring herself to voice: *for I shall never see you again.*

As the ship sailed farther and farther out to sea, Damien also remembered the letter he had written to his family, just before he left on this great journey:

"My dear family, be brave in doing God's will always and everywhere. This is the path that leads to heaven."

It was the eighth crossing of the seas for the *R. W. Wood*, a tall, proud three-masted ship. The red, white, and blue flag of the kingdom of Hawaii unfurled gracefully in the breeze. The *R. W. Wood* was set on its course across the Atlantic toward the tip of South America and on to the South Pacific.

Four and a half months of sea travel lay ahead for the Sacred Hearts missionaries: priests, religious brothers and sisters. The world became a blur of blue sea and skies. It took some getting used to. Damien did the best he could to keep from getting seasick. Even if he sat very still, his brain still felt as if it were turning cartwheels. Walking around the ship was next to impossible.

Brother Damien was the first to recover, however, and gain his "sea legs." Ever eager to be of service to what he called their "floating community," he took on the chore of preparing for daily Mass. He even made the hosts that would be used for Communion. He looked after his own little community, as well as others on board who didn't recover as quickly from seasickness. He made sure that everyone had what they needed to get through each day. Being busy and helpful made the long difficult days seem shorter. In the evenings he continued his theology studies with Brother Clement and Brother Lievin.

Shortly after the ship rounded Cape Horn at the tip of South America, dark storms began to torment its course. Waves as high as mountains rose on all sides, dwarfing the mighty sea vessel and tossing it around as if it were a toy. The passengers were destined to days of sliding helplessly from one side of the ship to the other. The two sailors at the wheel had to be tied there, for at any moment they could have been swept into the sea as waves crashed unrelentingly over the deck.

The ship lurched and jerked day and night. Down below in the wet cabins, the missionaries prayed with everyone aboard: "Mary, Star of the Sea, pray for us. Mary, Hope of the Hopeless, hear our cry!"

Above the deafening roar of the ocean, Father Chretien addressed the frightened missionaries, "Captain Geerkin said that nothing but a miracle can save this ship. Let's begin nine days of special prayer for the miracle we all need so desperately."

Amazingly, on the ninth day of prayer the winds died down and the captain announced that the danger had passed! It was hard to believe that those peaceful waters had just hours before been rolling avalanches of death. Up on deck again, the

*At long last, Damien heard the words
they had all been waiting for: "Land ahead!"*

grateful missionaries chanted a song of praise called the *Te Deum.* The sailors bowed their heads with respect. This was one trip they would never forget. For a long time afterward, the sailors would remind one another of those missionaries who had prayed them through a storm!

At long last, on March 18, 1864, Damien heard the words they had all been waiting for: "Land ahead!"

"It would be impossible for me to tell you of the immense joy I felt, after five months of traveling, to see the new country where I will labor to bring people to God," Damien wrote to his parents. From a distance it was hard to tell just what this land was like. But the journey was over, and a new life was awaiting Brother Damien.

8

ALOHA

Never before had Damien seen anything like Hawaii. As the island grew closer he was awestruck at the magnificent colors that came into view. It seemed like a dream to him. Everything was luxuriantly green. Back home he had been accustomed to willow trees and oaks. Here, it was like the Garden of Eden from the Bible! Different kinds of fruit trees were everywhere. He tried to imagine the taste of each of them: mango, breadfruit, coconut ... Would he ever learn how to eat them? And the flowers—he had never experienced such colors and scents before.

The smiling people of the island welcomed the new missionaries with their characteristic welcoming *aloha* spirit. They draped the newcomers with leis made from exotic orchids, shiny kukui nuts, seashells, and fragrant ginger flowers. Damien was already beginning to feel at home.

Later, as he walked around with a guide, he got a better look at the terrain. "What is that beautiful flower called?" Damien inquired.

"That is a plumeria. Smell the sweetness?" his guide picked the flower. Damien took a deep breath. He had never smelled a perfume like this before.

"We have *nothing* like this in my village!" Damien exclaimed.

"Your village must be very poor," his friend concluded with a chuckle.

I thought I came here to do great things, Damien reflected, *but great things like this fragrant flower are already here! Help me, Jesus, to learn everything about your beautiful islands and their people.*

Bishop Louis-Désiré Maigret was the bishop for the eight Hawaiian islands. When he met Damien in his rectory in Honolulu, the capital of Hawaii, he was immediately impressed by the brother's easygoing nature and enthusiastic spirit.

Damien was full of questions about his new mission home. "Can you tell me more about the good people here? I feel that the sooner I become familiar with their customs and language, the better I will be able to serve them."

The older man smiled at the young man's eagerness, "I can see you're off to a good start, Brother Damien. Soon I believe you will know and love them all as I do. The Hawaiians are a very friendly people, kind-hearted and always ready to forgive. Wait until you hear their music and join in their ceremonies. That's how they strengthen their faith and make Jesus a part of their everyday lives."

Damien listened attentively as the bishop described life on the Hawaiian Islands. Through the window in the bishop's office, Damien could see people passing by: bronze-skinned, dark-haired Hawaiians with soft, brilliant eyes and warm smiles. Their muscular build showed they were used to hard work. When he had passed them on the streets, even complete strangers waved at him! Damien already felt accepted here. *Yes, these are my people, too,* he thought.

The bishop soon decided that Damien was ready for the priesthood. On May 21, 1864, Damien was ordained a priest forever, along with Brother Clement and Brother Lievin. Damien was twenty-four years old and had been in Hawaii for just two months. As he knelt in the cathedral after the ceremony, he thanked God. He looked at his hands—strong hands that had once plowed and tilled a farm far away at home

in Tremelo. Now they were newly conse-
crated hands that would hold the Body and
Blood of his Lord and God, hands that
would be raised to absolve the sins of his
fellow men and women. Father Damien
buried his head in those hands and prayed,
"Make me worthy, O Lord!" In silence he
felt tears of joy well up in his eyes.

Slowly he rose and genuflected before
the Blessed Sacrament. If this moment had
happened in Tremelo, he would have
turned to meet his aged father and mother,
his family, and the townspeople, their faces
filled with joy and pride. But he was met
instead by islanders whose names he didn't
yet know. In spite of that, they welcomed
him with joy. These were the people of the
land to which he was dedicating his life.

The day after his ordination, Father
Damien celebrated his first Mass. In awe, he
held the chalice and the host that became
the Body and Blood of Jesus in his hands. "I
thought my heart would burst with joy the
first time I distributed the Bread of Life," he
wrote later.

Young Father Damien didn't have to
wait long for his first assignment. He and
Father Clement were to live on the largest
island, Hawaii, after which the entire island

group was later named. Damien's parish was to be the beautiful district of Puna. Damien put his whole heart into his new work. He also spent many hours mastering the Hawaiian language. After serving there for only a few months, Father Damien moved to a much larger part of the island, Kohala-Hamakua (pronounced *koh-HAH-lah hah-mah-COO-wah*). His new parish covered an area of more than a thousand square miles.

Damien wrote to his family in Belgium, "Don't forget me—your new priest—who, like the Good Shepherd, is now going out day and night on the volcanoes of the Hawaiian Islands in search of stray sheep. Pray for me day and night and ask others to pray for me." He needed their prayerful support more than ever as he navigated this new and exciting terrain. How he longed to bring the Gospel to those who awaited the Lord's message of love!

9

FIRE AND WATER

"Kamiano! Kamiano! Come quickly!"

Alarmed, Father Damien—by now accustomed to hearing the Hawaiian version of his name, Kamiano—leaped to his feet. What his people dreaded and feared the most had happened! For days now slight tremors had shaken the earth. They were the first signs of an impending volcanic eruption. And today it had come: the earth split open and rivers of fiery lava began to flow through the villages, burying everything in their paths. Smoke and ash filled the air.

The earthquake caused massive tsunamis which washed away entire villages in the Kohala district. Father Damien and many of the villagers were able to flee to safety in another village. But what would they find on their return?

"Kamiano, it has been days now … My husband was near the beach when the first tidal wave hit our village. I have not seen him since. He may be hurt. What am I going to do?" a frightened mother asked. A child of three or four clung to her side.

"As soon as it is safe, we will begin searching for survivors," Father Damien replied, trying to sound more hopeful than he felt. He had heard reports that the worst was over now. They could soon go home.

When the danger had subsided, Father Damien and his parishioners returned to the devastated area, carrying supplies to care for those who had been injured. Nearly one hundred people had died in the disaster. Damien surveyed the destruction in silence: during the past six years he had led the community in building the churches, schools, and homes that had been destroyed. And now everything—the fruits of their labor and patience—had been reduced to ashes.

Taking a deep breath, Father Damien gathered up his courage, "We will begin again, together!" he encouraged his people.

And begin again they did. Chapels and schools and homes rose up again.

"The people are amazed," the bishop commented to a fellow priest, "to see Father Damien coming down from the mountains carrying heavy logs for construction." But this kind of hard work came naturally to Damien. His experience on the family farm in Tremelo was finally coming in handy!

And that was what made the people grow to love this good young priest. He made himself one of them. He wasn't afraid to dirty his hands, and he was never too busy to serve them.

Two years after the eruption, everything had been rebuilt. There was little trace left of the volcano's devastation. Greatly satisfied, Father Damien wrote to Father Pamphile, who was back in Belgium, "This year I think I will be able to spend more time helping the sick in my parish, and maybe even studying, if the Lord doesn't send me elsewhere." Whether Damien suspected it or not, the Lord *was* preparing to send him elsewhere. And being the kind of man he was, Father Damien was ready for the challenge!

On the nearby island of Maui (pronounced *MAU-wee*), a fellow missionary, Father Leonor, had just completed building a new church. Bishop Maigret, making plans to bless it, invited all the priests in the area who were available.

Father Damien felt secure in leaving his parish for a while. The chapels were built. He even had catechists and prayer leaders who could carry on while he was away.

As the ship pulled away from Hawaii, Father Damien later confessed, "In my heart

I felt that I would never return, and would never again see my beloved parishioners or the beautiful chapels I had built. It brought tears to my eyes to leave this place which I had grown to love in the eight years I lived there."

A new chapter was beginning in the life of Father Damien—one that *nothing* could prepare him for!

10

A CRY FOR HELP

It was good to see the familiar faces of
his fellow priests again and to talk with his
superior, Father Modeste. The dedication of
the new church was a beautiful event for
both the priests and the people. In the little
reception hall, all the missionaries gathered,
reliving old times, exchanging news from
Europe, and, best of all, sharing the work
and successes of their own territories.

"Yes," said Bishop Maigret, "we can
thank God that much has been accom-
plished. New churches have been constructed. Hundreds of good people have been
baptized. Only God knows *all* the good
done by each of you. But one place still
needs our help ..."

The hall went still. All eyes were focused
on the Bishop. They knew the place he was
referring to: Molokai (pronounced *moh-loh-
KAH-ee*)—the island of the much-feared
disease of leprosy. This affliction was also
called the "death before death" because of
its terrible symptoms.

Leprosy had first struck the islands some thirty years before Damien's arrival. Panic and fear prompted difficult and drastic decisions. Because leprosy was thought to be highly contagious, King Kamehameha V (pronounced *kah-MEH-hah-MEH-hah*) made a law of segregation in 1865. All those diagnosed were separated from the rest of society and sent to Molokai, far away from their families and friends.

Scientists now know that leprosy—which is now called Hansen's disease—is caused by bacteria that infect a person's nerves. Untreated, leprosy can cause deformity and lifelong suffering. No one knows for sure how leprosy is spread, but scientists have discovered that it is not as highly contagious as people once thought. Today, Hansen's disease can be treated and even cured with antibiotics. But in Damien's time, doctors were only just beginning to understand this disease.

The king's law of segregation had devastating results. Families were pried apart and no one was exempt once a diagnosis was reported. Hansen's disease became known as the "separating sickness." Many hearts were broken. Being sent to Molokai was a terrible sentence.

No one knew exactly how many sick people were living on Molokai. Medicine and provisions were shipped irregularly and hastily dumped on the shore. Periodically a priest would visit, too, but that wasn't very often. Contact with the outside world was extremely limited. But the desperate pleas of those who lived with this disease, as well as those of their sorrowing families, had reached the ears of the bishop.

And so Bishop Maigret continued to explain the situation to his priests, "The people of our parish—yes, *our* parish—on Molokai are crying out, 'It isn't enough for us to see a priest once a year!'"

Father Damien heard nothing else. That heartbreaking plea for aid had to be answered. He couldn't drive it out of his mind. These good and desperate people were infinitely precious to the heart of God. At any cost they had to be helped!

So lost was Damien in this ocean of thoughts that he didn't notice the bishop beginning to walk around the assembly of priests. He had stopped to greet four of the youngest, and Father Damien was among them.

"I am heartbroken about Molokai." The bishop's words brought Damien back to reality. "The number of people in the settlement is growing constantly. No area in the islands needs a priest more. But ..." the bishop hesitated.

All four of the priests spoke up at once using almost the same words, "We'll go!"

Bishop Maigret was thunderstruck. What selfless generosity! Looking at them, he thought for a moment. "Well, your parishes need you, too. Right?" They nodded. "So how about taking turns—the four of you, three months each. Then our friends at Molokai will have a priest all year round." The entire group applauded. A perfect solution for a very difficult problem!

The four priests could easily take turns on Molokai. That way the burden would be divided. Father Damien volunteered to be the first. And it was his secret hope that somehow he'd be able to stay.

Not long after, the steamer *Kilauea* (pronounced *kee-lah-ooo-WAY-yah*) left the island of Maui, bound for Molokai. Bishop Maigret and Father Damien were on board. They were not alone. There were fifty sick people on board as well. As the ship set out into the blue waters, a cascade of blossoms was tossed from the shore. The grief-stricken families on shore, already overcome by loneliness, waved farewell to their loved ones—never to see them again. Father Damien watched the people on the ship sadly. To think that these people would be forced to spend the rest of their lives on Molokai, just because they were sick! It wasn't fair.

The bishop saw that the young priest was sad. He asked somewhat cautiously, "Are you sure about this, Father Damien?" Damien looked his bishop in the eyes.

"Even more sure than I was before," the young missionary replied emphatically.

11

MOLOKAI: DAY ONE

Stepping onto the shores of Molokai for the first time, Father Damien prayed for courage. Setting his few possessions down in the sand, he turned to watch the *Kilauea* sail away, becoming smaller and smaller on the horizon. Soon it was nothing more than a speck. Listening to the gentle sound of the waters lapping the beach, Damien became aware of other sounds nearby—a rustling whisper, a flurry of movement. Instantly, the parting advice of the bishop came into his mind: *Whatever you do, don't let people think you are afraid!* Damien closed his eyes and swallowed hard.

Slowly he turned to meet his new parishioners. They were hesitant, hanging back half-concealed in the bushes near the beach. They began to approach carefully, emerging silently as they surrounded their new priest.

For the first time, Father Damien felt very much alone and afraid. As he looked around he thought, *This can't be ... these people must suffer so much!*

The islanders surrounding him had at one time undoubtedly been strong and handsome and graceful. Now, all traces of former beauty were gone, lost to the disfiguring power of the painful disease. Some were shrunken with leprosy, others swollen with it—but all were deformed. Wounds covered their broken bodies, bandaged by scraps of fabric, testifying to the longtime neglect they had suffered.

It took all Damien's inner strength to pull himself together. He forced himself to smile, a gesture many of these people rarely saw. Their own mouths were often too pain-racked to smile. Besides, a smile must begin in the heart, and these ostracized, forgotten people were not smiling on the inside *at all*. It would take much to change this.

After a brief tour of the unkept wooden shacks that they lived in, Father Damien set to work that very afternoon. One of his first priorities was the chapel, which was about to fall apart. If he was going to help these people spiritually, he needed a place for all of them to come together.

"Give me the strength I do not have myself," he prayed as he knelt on the dusty altar steps. "Divine Heart of Jesus, teach me how to love this neglected parish of yours."

Rising, he rolled up his sleeves and began to attack the dust and cobwebs all around the chapel. A few hours of silent labor passed. Suddenly Father Damien noticed a shadow blocking the sunlight from the door. He looked up. A man was standing just outside, his body afflicted by the advanced stages of the disease. Slowly extending his hand, he said, "A gift for you, Father." Surprised, Damien got up and went out into the sun to speak with him. A beautiful ripe mango was resting in the man's heavily bandaged hands.

The common wisdom of his time would have urged Damien to turn away and refuse the man's gift. What if it had been contaminated by the disease? But Father Damien was determined to show how much he cared for his new parishioners. He didn't want to set himself apart from them, even if it meant risking his own well-being. He reminded himself, *I'm here to help and serve these good people, no matter the cost.*

So Damien's response was immediate and meaningful. Overcoming his hesitation, he gratefully took the gift. The surprise and relief in the eyes of his visitor were priceless. Biting into the mango, Damien smiled his gratitude. The man ran as fast as he could to

*I'm here to help and serve these good people,
no matter the cost.*

tell his friends about this new pastor, the priest who was not afraid to be among them. In time, Damien came to understand that this was a type of test for newcomers to Molokai: Damien would be measured from then on by this one moment.

Later that same day, some of the women arrived with bouquets of flowers that they had gathered to make the little chapel beautiful once more. They began to help the young priest with some of the cleaning. Suddenly, a villager burst in. "Father, please come quickly! A friend has died." Damien dropped what he was doing. Wiping his hands on his clothes, he quickly followed his guide.

But when they reached the cemetery, Damien couldn't believe what he saw. Death was such a common occurrence on Molokai that there was no special treatment for those who had died. The body was simply dumped in a shallow ditch without a coffin and covered with a light blanket of earth. No prayers, no flowers, no mark of respect or love followed these villagers to their graves. Damien realized that this also posed a significant health hazard, for even more diseases could be spread as the bodies decayed. Plans began to form in his mind.

He had never made a coffin before, but what did it matter? With help, he could learn.

Returning from the cemetery, he felt a slight tug on his cassock. Turning, he saw an old woman bent over with sorrow. "My son is dying," she cried softly. "Could you come and see him?"

"Please, show me where you live," Damien urged. The two went together. Damien barely noticed the guava trees or flowers as he followed the path only the woman could find. They finally came to the shelter in a small clearing. She led him inside to meet her son. The twisted form of the young man, the dire poverty of the home, and the darkness that filled the room fueled new determination in the priest. *I have to do something about this*, thought Damien. He remained in the house, praying, until the boy died.

On his way back to the chapel, Damien thought, *I'd need ten lifetimes to make a difference here. Lord, what can I do? How can I help these people in only three short months?*

As the sun began to set, the young priest realized how tired he was. *I've got to get some sleep*, he thought. Then it dawned on him. *I don't have a house! I don't even have a bed! I'm not sure there's even a place to get clean water here.* In a moment of terror, Damien realized the scope of his commitment to this new mission. He closed his eyes and calmed his nerves, and with a deep breath said a quick prayer. "Jesus, you had no place to put your head, either. I know you are here with me and will never abandon me. Give me strength."

He walked back to the shore, where he came upon a large pandanus tree. "This will be my house," he said with a smile. For a time, the branches of the tree would be his only shelter. Eventually he would build a house. But first, he had more important challenges to face.

12

HERE TO STAY

Aole kanawai me keia wahi.

These words sent a chill through the young priest's heart. They were the motto of a hopeless people: "In this place there is no law." Many people on Molokai saw no future for themselves. Trapped on the island with no hope of escape, they began to think that it no longer mattered how they treated themselves—or others.

Father Damien was deeply concerned about this spirit of lawlessness. Nights on Molokai were by no means peaceful or silent. The heartrending wails and groans of the sick were to be expected. But the drunken laughter and wild celebrations that often filled the evening air spoke of the desperation that reigned on the island.

One evening, while trying to navigate the local terrain, Father Damien came upon one of these out-of-control parties. When the crowd caught sight of his cassock, the frightened cry arose, "Father Damien!" People scattered in all directions to avoid being recognized by their pastor. A few hid behind the trees, waiting to see what Father Damien would do.

The young priest strode out of the forest, clearing away the wooden cups of liquor left abandoned in the panic. "You may think there is no law on Molokai, but the law of God is for everyone to follow!" His words rang out in the darkness. Damien's display of courage made enemies for him that night.

The following day everything seemed fine—at least on the surface. "You know, many are unhappy with your presence here, Father," a man named Michael confided to him.

Father Damien continued to hammer on the casket he was finishing. "Yes, I'm aware of that."

"They may even try to hurt you," he stammered nervously.

The priest smiled, "Now, Michael. What could they ever do to hurt me?"

"Father," Michael pleaded, "no police have ever been effective here. We have a weapon that *everyone* is afraid of."

"What's that?" Damien stopped what he was doing, wiping sweat on his sleeve as he listened to his friend.

Michael cleared his throat and whispered, "Our disease."

It was true. Fear of catching the disease was sometimes used against outsiders. But Father Damien was a different kind of man. The people of Molokai soon saw that he wasn't afraid of the leprosy that affected them. He ate their food, drank from their cups, and even shared his pipe with them. No one had ever seen anyone like him before!

In 1873 he wrote home to Tremelo in words that became a motto of his life on Molokai: "My greatest happiness is to serve the Lord in these people made outcasts by their fellow human beings."

Father Damien's efforts did not escape the notice of Bishop Maigret and Father Modeste, his superior. They both agreed that Father Damien's presence on Molokai was bringing very good results. And they both knew how much he desired to remain on Molokai and to devote his whole life to the people there. His letters to them were sprinkled with plans and projects, and it was obvious this energetic young missionary had the strong will to carry them through to completion.

In July 1873, Father Damien went to Honolulu to receive the good news of his permanent assignment to Molokai. What a happy heart he had on his return! The people knew and felt they had found a true friend. A wave of hope spread through the colony. They were no longer orphans!

13

THE "MIRACLE" OF WATER

The locals called Molokai the "land of the cliffs." Its jagged gray mountains formed forbidding walls that cut off a small peninsula from the rest of the island. It was here on this isolated point of land that the two colonies called Kalawao (pronounced *kah-lah-WAH-oh*) and Kalaupapa (pronounced *kah-LAH-oo-PA-pa*) were located. There was a superintendent of the colony, a man by the name of Meyer, but he lived on another part of the island. So the burden of both the spiritual and physical needs of the people fell on the young priest's shoulders.

Early each morning, Father Damien left his shelter beneath the pandanus tree. His strong, black-clad form could be seen at prayer for several hours in the little chapel dedicated to Saint Philomena. Then he would say Mass. He received his inner strength from this daily time with Jesus. Then he would set to work. Each day there was much to be done to improve life in the settlement.

"Michael," Father Damien said one day, "I have an idea. But I'm going to need your help."

Michael shaded his weak eyes from the bright Hawaiian sun. He could see the young priest's eager face. "Father, I know that look ... what are you thinking of?"

"We need water, Michael."

"Water? We have very little of that, I'm afraid," his friend apologized.

Father Damien put his hand gently on Michael's sore shoulder and pointed to the mountains around them. "There have to be mountain streams up there somewhere," he reasoned. "We need *that* water. Our colony will be a cleaner and happier place to live in."

An expedition on foot proved the missionary's conclusion. At the end of the valley of Waihanau (pronounced *why-hah-NAH-oo*) they found a seventy-foot-wide pool of ice-cold water, clear and sparkling. But water in the mountains did no good to anyone down in the settlement, so Father Damien got to work. He sent letters, first to the board of health and then to influential friends living in Honolulu. And these brought wonderful results.

One day, a ship landed at Molokai. Its cargo? A good supply of strong water pipes.

The priest was ecstatic. "Michael!" he called to his faithful friend. "Call everyone who is able to help. We're going to need many extra hands today!"

But it was a disappointed Michael who came back to inform Father Damien that there were no volunteers. "My people are without hope. They are too used to living with death to believe there can ever be improvement in their lives."

Father Damien was undaunted. He personally went from shack to shack—pleading, persuading, promising—inviting people to join him in his endeavor. He whispered a prayer to Jesus: "Help me, Lord, to find the words that will give my people the courage to make this pipeline happen."

The young priest who spoke with energy and vibrant persuasion lit a flame of hope in the village. The islanders banded together to unload the cargo. But that was just the beginning!

For several days, the work went on, each person doing what he or she could to help. Father Damien laid the pipes himself. His only guide was a memory of the plans he had sketched in the sand.

Finally, one morning, the work was completed. At long last, the villagers witnessed the miracle of running water. The pipes ran down to the village, where several taps were set up for people to use. Clean mountain water flowed into their jugs and buckets. Shouts of joy echoed through the colony as never before.

But Father Damien didn't wait around to be thanked. There was plenty more work to do! He continued his tasks of priest, doctor, gravedigger, and coffin maker, always looking ahead to plan more ways of making Molokai a real home for everyone.

14

OPPOSITION

Father Damien looked up at the neat brick building in Honolulu. Wouldn't it be wonderful to have houses like that on Molokai someday? But now he must make sure the facts were clear in his mind. Ahead was an appointment with the board of health—and only facts interested them.

It hadn't been easy for Father Damien to get an appointment with the president of the board of health. It was sad, but here he was unpopular. Many officials in Honolulu were jealous of the acclaim given to the young priest. It made them look bad— negligent, to say the least.

He was sent from secretary to secretary and finally back to the doorman—all in the hope of confusing him. He had to sign a paper here and answer questions there. Father Damien, however, was used to over-coming obstacles. "I came to see the president," he firmly declared, "and I will not leave until I have seen him!"

Father Damien finally got through to the president's office, but the official was not very cooperative. He sat comfortably behind his marble-topped desk.

"Please, sir," the priest pleaded, "my people must have better food and clothing. Some are still wearing what they had when they first came to Molokai ..."

The president idly toyed with his pen and sighed. "Remember, sir," he said finally, "these affairs do not concern you. You are a priest, and all you have to do is take care of the spiritual needs of those lepers. Mind your own business!"

That did it. Damien had had enough. He stood up. Until now he had restrained his temper, but love for his newfound family made him speak. He told the man exactly what he thought of officials who professed concern for the unfortunates of society, yet lived lives so contrary to their preaching.

"There's a law," the president replied angrily, "that it seems you have forgotten. *No one* from the colony may *ever* leave it."

"*You* have forgotten that I do not have leprosy," Father Damien answered.

"But you live at the settlement," the other man almost shouted. "If you ever leave Molokai again, or even leave that part of the island and cross those mountains, you will be arrested!"

The young priest was not intimidated. "When I need to see my bishop," he responded firmly, "I will see him. When I wish to visit the other Catholics on Molokai who do *not* have leprosy, I *will* visit them."

In a rage, the president left the room.

Back on Molokai once more, the missionary knelt in the little chapel, pouring out his soul to the only One who truly understands and sees all things. Visiting Honolulu hadn't been a total loss. The bishop himself had collected new supplies for the colony, and public sympathy had been stirred as well. A welcome shipment of lumber would soon land on this desolate part of the island. But why, when there was dire need, did so many other people have to block the way with technicalities?

"I do not understand, Lord," he prayed, "but give me strength. You were opposed, too. Help me hold on to you no matter what."

The opposition, however, was just beginning. The next ship brought a letter from the board of health, forbidding anyone to leave or land on Molokai, under penalty of arrest!

15

GOD NEVER LEAVES HIS OWN

In spite of this opposition, Molokai was changing. Much progress had been made. With the new lumber, shabby huts had been replaced by small, tidy cottages. The missionary even encouraged the residents to plant gardens around their homes, trusting that even small improvements would make hope grow in their own hearts. Slowly attitudes started shifting. The people took an interest in themselves now, and as they did so, life seemed more bearable.

Reform on Molokai had changed the outlook on death, too. Father Damien, who got his strength from the thought of heaven, tried to help his parishioners understand that death was the beginning of a new and eternal life with God.

"Father," one elderly woman confided, "I'm not so afraid to think of dying now. You said that when we rise one day, our bodies will be beautiful again." Her eyes filled with tears. "We have forgotten what it was like to be beautiful." Father Damien watched her hobble away.

A blend of ingenuity and concern gave Father Damien a wonderful idea. He organized a burial society. The members made uniforms and colorful banners. When a fellow villager died, they made the funeral as solemn and as beautiful as they could. They carried the person's body in procession, singing and honoring it as a temple of the Holy Spirit. This brought hope to all the villagers.

But in the midst of all this progress, Father Damien still had deep personal sufferings. Loneliness is a painful thing for anyone to experience. It was even more so for Father Damien, a man so strong and healthy, living on an island that the outside world called a "graveyard." Damien also missed the peace and strength that comes from the sacrament of Reconciliation. Because he was the only priest on Molokai, he often had to go for long periods of time without being able to participate in this sacrament. He had always been honest and upright when it came to his conscience. Damien knew he had a temper and worked hard to be kind and gentle. He knew he needed the Lord's mercy just as much as the people he served.

One day, a small ship anchored offshore brought more people who had been diagnosed with leprosy. It was the priest's custom to meet the new arrivals, no matter how busy he was. Damien understood how terrifying that first moment on the unfamiliar island could be. But this particular morning he almost forgot to welcome his new charges as he looked out at the ship, for his superior stood on the deck, waving.

"Father Modeste!" he shouted excitedly. Leaping into a canoe with two men, Father Damien paddled out to the ship's side.

"You can't go ashore," he suddenly heard the captain bark at Father Modeste. "I have my orders from the board of health."

Father Modeste objected, "But he's my fellow priest. He doesn't have leprosy. I only want to visit him."

The captain stalked away. "Orders are orders! I'm sorry," he said over his shoulder.

Shocked, Father Modeste gazed over the ship's rail at his spiritual brother. Despite the glimmering sunlight, the young priest could read the helpless fury in his superior's eyes. Father Damien swallowed hard. The memory of the board's decree came back to him. But he was used to obstacles.

"Father," Damien called out, "does anyone else on board understand French?"

"No one but me, Damien."

Father Damien shielded his eyes from the sun and looked up at Father Modeste. "Then I will go to Confession right here," he declared. "I may not have the chance again for a long time."

And so the young missionary knelt in the canoe and confessed his sins. Above the roaring of the surf, his voice rang out in French. The sailors and the islanders watched in silent respect. They admired this young priest whose love for God was greater than his pride.

"I absolve you ..." Father Modeste raised his hand and traced the sign of the cross over Damien. A divine peace settled over Father Damien's soul—peace from Jesus himself.

He rose and waved farewell as the ship pulled anchor and began to head toward open seas. *How true*, he thought, *that God never leaves his own.* Ahead would still be days of trial, hard work, and, no doubt, more loneliness, but he had God's strength with him. Who could be against him?

16

VISIT FROM A PRINCESS

The burial society, a choir, a hospital, and a boys' home—all the improvements in Kalawao and Kalaupapa—had come about through hard work, sacrifice, and long hours of prayer.

From Father Damien's anxious, elderly mother in Tremelo came a pleading letter: "My son, be careful. Don't expose yourself imprudently to this disease. Don't over-work. I love you and follow you with my prayers."

From the eager missionary came the reply: "I love you, too, Mama. Please don't worry. I live well. I have my two meals a day at home. For breakfast I have rice, sometimes meat, and coffee with a few biscuits. In the evening I dine on what is left over from the morning, with a cup of tea made from water I boil over my little lamp."

Father Damien didn't tell his mother that his noon meal was in the home of a person who had leprosy. All his life the missionary was criticized for this "imprudence." But *was* it imprudence? Damien didn't think so.

Damien's first priority was to ensure that the people of Molokai felt loved and accepted by him.

Each evening a group of villagers would seat themselves on Damien's rectory floor and chat with him. They would beg him to tell them stories of faraway Europe or about his family in Tremelo. When he received letters from his parents, the little circle of visitors wouldn't leave until Damien had translated every word for them. And the gatherings never ended until the pipe of friendship had been passed. The pipe was passed from mouth to mouth, touching mouths blistering with sores, mouths that often had no recognizable lips at all. Father Damien shared in the gesture, for they truly were his friends, and he'd never insult them or hurt their feelings by refusing.

His dedication was known beyond Molokai, even by Hawaiian royalty. In 1881, the King of Hawaii was traveling. Princess Liliuokalani (pronounced *lee-lee-OO-who-kah-lah-nee*) governed in his absence. She had always wanted to visit Molokai, and now was her chance!

*Princess Liliuokalani had always wanted
to visit Molokai, and this was her chance!*

Eight hundred villagers waited eagerly on the beach for the arrival of the princess. They were dressed in their finest clothes, the uniforms of the burial society. Flower-covered canopies were constructed to cover the princess and her attendants.

When she stepped onto the sands of Molokai for the very first time, Princess Liliuokalani looked around and saw a sea of faces, all smiling respectfully. Father Damien stepped forward to greet her.

"So you are the man who has done so much to relieve the suffering of my people," she said gratefully.

Father Damien had never dealt with royalty before. "I love them," he explained.

The princess smiled graciously and turned to her attendant, "I wish to see the whole settlement."

"But, Your Highness," the attendant objected, "it may be too much for you ..."

Princess Liliuokalani wasn't listening. She was already walking, with Father Damien as her guide.

In the hour allotted for her visit, the princess toured the entire settlement. She felt immense compassion for these people who knew so much suffering. Her attendants hung back from entering the hospital, even though it was their duty to accompany the princess everywhere. But not Liliuokalani. Her heart was torn with pity as she gazed on the people lying on mats at her feet. Groans and sighs surrounded her, and the smell of decay drowned out the sweet perfume she wore.

As she stood once again on the beach, a surprise was offered to her by the islanders. Horns, flutes, and drums, all donated by benefactors, were brought out, and the new band of Molokai began to play. Some of the members heroically managed to blow through lips that were only partially there, while others had to pause occasionally to catch their breath, but the music was beautiful, accompanied by the singing of those who could not play.

With tears in her eyes, the princess bid farewell to these good people and then turned to Father Damien. He bent to kiss her hand, knowing no other gesture to make at such a moment.

"You are so good," her voice was choked. "You are so strong and healthy, yet you have given your life for these people. I admire you, sir."

"But they're my flock ..." he explained, a bit embarrassed to use the words used by the Good Shepherd himself.

"Your flock," she interrupted, touched by emotion, "and *my people*."

The royal ship finally departed, growing smaller on the horizon, and Damien was once again left alone with his parish. But not for long ...

After the princess' visit, the board of health was forced to relax the strict law that stopped people from visiting the colony. This allowed other priests and doctors to visit the settlements once in a while. Damien was thrilled to be able to see his religious superior once again.

Shortly after Princess Liliuokalani's departure, Bishop Maigret arrived in Kalaupapa. He brought a jeweled cross with him, a gift from the princess to Father Damien. It was an award naming him Knight Commander of the Royal Order of Kalakaua (pronounced *kah-LAH-KAH-oo-wah*). The aged bishop watched the young priest as he examined the medal, then casually set it down.

He isn't doing this for fame, thought the bishop with a smile. He knew there was only one insignia that Father Damien ever took pride in: the Sacred Hearts emblem that was part of his religious habit.

17

THE WAY OF THE CROSS

It was a hot afternoon in 1884. Damien was forty-four years old. No breeze came to relieve the perspiring little settlement. Not a leaf stirred. As he sat in his stuffy confessional waiting for penitents, Damien inwardly resolved to infuse extra courage into whoever would come today. A few minutes later the familiar sound of shuffling steps and thumping canes started to fill the chapel.

Father Damien had always had to remind himself to be patient when hearing confessions on these long afternoons. With the fearful he was gentle, with others he was firm, but he tried always to be compassionate.

Patiently, Father Damien listened as people shared their discouragement, their fear, their loneliness. He promised each one his prayers, assuring them that there *was* a heaven to hope for, something that he repeated over and over. He reminded his people that this life is like a breath compared to the eternity of perfect happiness that lies ahead and that through our suffering we share in the cross of Jesus.

After celebrating the sacrament of Reconciliation with one of his parishioners, Father Damien often gave the person a favorite penance, which was his own, too: making the Way of the Cross. Through this prayer, the person was invited to reflect on the last moments of Jesus' life and to remember how much Jesus suffered for love of each of us. The Way of the Cross ended with a hope-filled reminder of the glorious resurrection to come.

Three hours later, coming from the confessional, Father Damien paused to kneel for a moment before the tabernacle before going home.

"All day long," he had written to Father Pamphile, "I am surrounded by all kinds of physical and spiritual miseries which break my heart. Nevertheless, I try to be cheerful, so that I might encourage others ..."

Today had been one of those days. His head throbbed and his tired body ached. He decided to finish reading his prayer book while he soaked his feet. He sat back, picked up his worn prayer book, and began to read.

Through the evening air, he could hear the people singing, as they often did at night. This was a beloved custom with Hawaiians at family or village gatherings. Tonight they were singing a chant that had become a favorite on Molokai. As the soft strains reached his ears, he paused to listen. He never became tired of it. The words reminded him of a psalm he prayed often: *With all my heart, I am waiting for you, Lord!*

Suddenly the clock struck ten. Father Damien took his feet out of the basin to dry them. He stopped the towel in midair and stared at his blistered feet. Blistered ... but why was that? He reached down to test the water with one finger. To his horror, it was still scalding. And he hadn't felt it ... He leaned back in the chair and closed his eyes. Loss of feeling was one of the first signs of the disease—leprosy.

There was a specialist visiting the sick at this time, and the next day Father Damien paid him a visit.

When he had finished examining the missionary, Dr. Arning sat down and pretended to shuffle through some papers on the desk.

"Doctor," the priest said, "what is it?"

There were a few moments of hesitation. Then Dr. Arning looked up to measure his patient's courage. "What you think is true," he said in a low voice. "I'm so sorry."

The shock that each member his parish had experienced had now been dealt to their pastor. But Father Damien didn't object. Calmly he answered, "I knew it. I expected it would happen, from the first day I came to Molokai."

To his superior in Honolulu he wrote, "There is no doubt. I now have leprosy, too. Blessed be the good God! Please don't feel too sorry for me. But please send another priest to help me here and to be my confessor." And to the superior general of his community, living in Europe, he wrote: "Don't be too surprised or pained to hear that I am honored with not only the royal cross of the King of Hawaii, but also with a cross that is heavier—that of leprosy."

Back in Tremelo, aged Mama De Veuster died of sorrow on hearing of the illness that had struck her beloved Joseph.

18

BLESSED MARIANNE COPE

The world reacted strongly to the news that Father Damien had contracted leprosy. Those who loved him were shocked, and they resolved to help him even more. Those who disliked him blamed this misfortune on his lack of caution. They said he was foolish. They said he just wanted publicity.

But a little group of religious sisters in Honolulu couldn't have cared less what newspapers and journals were saying about the apostle of Molokai. For two years these Franciscan sisters had operated a branch hospital on the Honolulu coast for people in the first stages of leprosy. Father Damien had wanted the sisters to come to Molokai, but the board of health had blocked his plans. But as it happened, the sisters were soon to have Father Damien as one of their own patients. It was nearly two years since he had been diagnosed, and Damien was coming to try one of the new treatments for leprosy discovered by Dr. Masanao Goto, a Japanese physician who had done research into leprosy.

"Sister Leopoldina, there's a spot up there near the ceiling you missed," Mother Marianne pointed out, stepping carefully around the ladder where Sister Leopoldina was perched with a paintbrush.

"Where? It looks fine to me!" she asked, searching for the spot.

"To your right, about a foot from where you were," Mother explained.

Sister Leopoldina carefully moved the ladder and touched up the corner.

"You've got it!" exclaimed Mother Marianne. "I think this room is just about ready for our guest."

The sisters had prepared for Damien's arrival with great care. Standing back, Mother Marianne inspected the little room he was to occupy. "Clean sheets, towels, a water basin," she observed. "Ah, yes. The most important thing is missing."

Sister Leopoldina wondered what could have been forgotten as Mother left the room. In a flash she reappeared carrying a crucifix. "But Mother," Sister Leopoldina exclaimed in surprise. "It's the one from your room."

Mother smiled. "I know. But Father Damien will need this now more than ever," she said. "While you have the ladder, could you hang it up for me?"

To the sisters, Father Damien was a hero. His sickness didn't repulse or frighten them. They looked upon him as a soldier wounded in battle for the sake of others. When they finally welcomed him, it was compassion and not horror that they felt so deeply.

He was only in his forties, but his hard life had aged him. His hair, once jet black, was lined with gray. Behind thick lenses, his eyes, already quite weak, were red and watery. The tropical sun had taken its toll, but the disease further worsened his vision. The leprosy had begun to distort his face, too. Once handsome, Damien's face was now tinged with purple, his nose and ears swollen.

Father Damien was not accustomed to being served. And the continual thought of his poor villagers back in Molokai tormented him. What if some should die without his ministry? He was also eager to introduce Dr. Goto's treatment for leprosy to his people in Molokai.

"I cannot be away from Molokai any longer," he announced to Mother Marianne one day as they sat talking.

"Yes, I know," she smiled sympathetically. She understood the heart of this apostle. She shared his concerns, too.

"But before I go, please promise to send some sisters to Molokai. There are children there who need a mother's love and care. And we badly need a home for the orphaned girls."

"Molokai is our dream, Father," Mother Marianne nodded. "We will come as soon as we can."

His parting words left a deep impression on her, "Please hurry, Mother. There isn't much time, you know."

Mother Marianne Cope wasn't easily discouraged.

She had been born two years before Damien, in Heppenheim, Germany, and baptized as Barbara. In 1840, her family immigrated to Utica, New York. Barbara had felt the inspiration of God's love as a child and young adult. She worked for a time in a factory, but in her prayers she heard the Lord speak to her heart. He wanted something special of her. She often prayed to Saint Francis of Assisi, whom she regarded as a special patron, and eventually she joined the Franciscan Sisters in Syracuse, New York. Just as Joseph De Veuster changed his name

"Molokai is our dream, Father," Mother Marianne
said. "We will come as soon as we can."

to Damien when he became a religious brother, Barbara chose the name Marianne when she became a religious sister. Sister Marianne worked at various jobs as a teacher, nurse, and administrator. She was eventually appointed provincial superior of her community in 1877.

In June 1883, a letter arrived at Mother Marianne's desk. As she read it, her heart was moved. *What a mysterious and wonderful place Hawaii must be,* she thought.

Later, one of the sisters noticed that something seemed to be on her mind. "Mother Marianne, is there something wrong? You seem so distracted."

"Oh, I can't get this letter out of my mind. I feel the Lord may be asking something of me, though I'm not sure I can handle it."

"If the Lord wants it," smiled her friend, "he will go before you to light the way."

Yes, thought Mother Marianne, *I must trust his grace and light to be my strength.* She was forty-five years old and had belonged to the Sisters of Saint Francis for twenty-one years. Little did she suspect how much her life was about to change.

After much prayer and reflection, Mother Marianne decided to respond to the plea for help. A priest from Hawaii, Father Leonor Fouesnel, was asking the Sisters of Saint Francis to help establish much-needed hospitals in Hawaii. And so it was that five months later, in November 1883, seven Sisters of Saint Francis set foot on the beautiful island of Hawaii. Mother Marianne and her sisters were to manage the branch hospital Kakaako (pronounced *kah-kah-AH-koh*) on Oahu (pro-nounced *oh-AH-hoo*). This hospital served as a receiving station for leprosy patients from all over the islands, and there were already more than two hundred people awaiting help when the sisters arrived.

The sisters worked wonders for the people in the first two years they were there. "We need to do something for the children of our patients, especially the girls. When their parents become sick, there is often no one to look after them," explained Mother Marianne on a bright day filled with the fragrance of flowers.

"When you get that look, Mother, the sky's the limit," chuckled one sister. Soon a home for girls was established on the hospital grounds. The sisters were doing wonderful work—exactly what they had set out to do. But Father Damien still waited for help on Molokai. Their work was not yet done...

19

HELPING HANDS

Damien returned to Molokai after being cared for by the sisters, and he immediately resumed his work. His pace was not slowed; in fact he doubled it. Aware that his days were numbered, he worked fiercely among the people to be sure that they would be provided for when he was no longer with them. But now Father Damien was no longer alone. As news of his efforts had spread, help began to arrive in Molokai.

On July 29, 1886, Joseph Dutton landed on Molokai. A convert to the Catholic faith and a veteran of the Civil War, he had heard about Father Damien's efforts on Molokai and had decided to dedicate the rest of his life to this work, too. When he arrived, Damien was thrilled. The ideas and plans of the tall, soldierly American added new vigor to the priest.

The two men worked well together. Father Damien even called Joseph "Brother" Dutton. Brother Dutton helped in all kinds of tasks, from gardening to finishing coffins.

He gently cared for the sick and also helped Father Damien with his bookkeeping.

Later they were joined by James Sinnett from Chicago, who became known as Brother James. From England came the help of an Anglican minister, the Reverend Hugh B. Chapman. He had taken up collections, sending the money to Molokai with the message: "You have taught me more by the story of your life than all the books I have ever read."

"He keeps saying, 'There is so much left to do,'" Brother James said to Brother Dutton. "We'll never get him to slow down." Of all people, Dutton knew that was true. Together both these honorary brothers had tried to relieve the physical burdens of the priest as much as they could, but still Damien wouldn't slow down.

By this time, Father Damien's nose had completely collapsed, and breathing had become so difficult for him that he could only sleep for an hour or two each night. One of his eyes had also failed him, while the other grew steadily weaker. As Father

Damien celebrated Mass each morning, the two men would watch in concern.

In September 1888, a serious fever racked his body, confining him to bed. Brother James and Brother Dutton cared for him around the clock. Father Louis-Lambert Conrardy, a priest who had come to help on Molokai, was there as well.

Damien had been sick for six weeks when the news came that a wealthy banker, Charles Bishop, had donated $5,000 to the Hawaiian government for the purpose of building a home for girls on Molokai. Who better to oversee the project than Mother Marianne? Two sisters—Sister Leopoldina Burns and Sister Vincentia McCormick—offered to come with her to Molokai. To Father Damien's great joy, the sisters arrived in November. They ran their home for girls on Molokai with gentleness and love. They also lent their expertise to the home for boys that Father Damien had founded, and after his death, Mother Marianne was put in charge of this important work.

On December 17, 1888, a wealthy Englishman, Edward Clifford, also visited Molokai. Clifford was an artist. He wished to capture the hero of Molokai on canvas. It took some doing to persuade Father Damien to sit long enough for the artist to work.

When the painting was finished, Father Damien grimaced. "Oh … I didn't know I looked so ugly!" he remarked. "We don't have too much of a demand on Molokai for mirrors, you know." An awkward silence filled the room.

Clearing his throat, Clifford asked, "Father, may I send a copy to your brother, Pamphile? You haven't seen him for so long."

Father Damien was silent. His brother knew of Damien's illness, but that was enough. With a slight catch in his voice, Damien responded, "No, please. It would hurt him too much to see me this way."

It was clear that Molokai would soon bid farewell to its father and friend.

20

A LEGACY OF COMPASSION

There were now many people who would carry on the good works that Damien had begun on Molokai. He was no longer as worried about the welfare of the islanders for whom he had worked so long and hard. Father Wendelin Moellers, a priest of the Sacred Hearts, came to carry on Father Damien's work on Molokai. Letters of recognition arrived from all parts of the globe; collections were taken up; even doctors came to offer their services on the island of suffering! Father Damien was happy and at peace. At last, the world knew and cared about his family on Molokai!

"My day is done," he told his friends as they gathered around his sickbed. "I can die now. You will continue to carry on the work even better than I could." To these generous friends who had come to help him, he gave away all he had, which wasn't much.

On March 30, 1889, Father Wendelin heard Damien's confession, and then the two missionaries renewed their religious vows together. "Tell Father General," Father

Damien begged Father Wendelin, "how happy I am to die a member of the Congregation of the Sacred Hearts!"

"Yes, forever we serve Jesus and Mary," responded Father Wendelin. In his short time on the island, Father Wendelin had come to greatly admire Damien. After a time, Father Wendelin spoke again, "Damien, I hope you don't mind my asking, but may I keep your cloak?"

The dying priest, shaking with fever, brushed him off with a little smile and whispered, "What for? It's full of leprosy!"

On April 15, 1889, at the age of forty-nine, Father Damien died, resting like a little child in the arms of his faithful friend Brother James. Outside, the islanders sadly sang the song he had loved so much: *With all my heart, I am waiting for you, Lord!*

Grief overcame the villagers when they were told their father had died. They buried him under the pandanus tree where he had spent those first nights on Molokai. The great voice of their pastor was silent now; the strong body that had once built chapels, cottages, pipelines, and coffins was at rest.

He was gone from this earth, but people like Father Damien never die in our hearts. He proved by the way he lived that no sacrifice is too great for love. Father Damien made real the words of his Divine Master, taken from the Gospel of Saint John, carved on the monument erected in his memory:

"No one has greater love than this: to lay down one's life for one's friends."

Mother Marianne Cope remained on Molokai for the rest of her life, dedicated to continuing the important work begun by Damien. She died peacefully at the age of eighty. None of her sisters ever contracted the dread disease. On May 14, 2005, Mother Marianne—a true heroine of Hawaii—was declared blessed by the Church. Her feast day is celebrated each year on her birthday, January 23.

A statue now stands in Father Damien's honor in the National Statuary Hall in the U.S. Capitol in Washington, D.C.; another stands outside the Hawaii Capitol. He was beatified by Pope John Paul II in 1995. The universal Church rejoiced to celebrate the canonization of Saint Damien of Molokai on October 11, 2009. We celebrate his feast day each year on May 10—the day he first set foot on the shores of Molokai.

PRAYER

Saint Damien, you learned to love others with the heart of Jesus. You saw the dignity and beauty of each person you served, where others saw only pain and misery. You embraced a new land and culture and helped people to have new hope.

Pray for me that I might see others as Jesus sees them—as my brothers and sisters. May I recognize the needs of people around me and be willing to help, even when it is difficult, just as you did. When I experience challenges or suffering, pray for me that I may always be courageous and hope-filled. And may my own heart always be filled with the love of Jesus and Mary. Amen.

GLOSSARY

1. *aloha*—a Hawaiian word used as a greeting or to describe the friendliness and welcoming spirit of the islanders.

2. beatification—the ceremony in which the Catholic Church recognizes that a deceased person lived a life of Gospel holiness in a heroic way. In most cases, a proven miracle obtained through the holy person's prayers to God is also required. A person who is beatified is given the title Blessed.

3. breadfruit—a large round fruit that has a starchy texture similar to bread; it is native to the Pacific islands.

4. canonization—the ceremony in which the pope officially declares that someone is a saint in heaven. To canonize someone is to recognize that he or she has lived a life of heroic virtue, is worthy of imitation, and can intercede for others. Like beatification, which it follows, canonization requires a miracle resulting from the holy person's prayers to God.

5. cassock—full-length robe (often black) that may be worn by priests.

6. **contagion**—the means by which an infectious disease is spread, such as bacteria or a virus.

7. **guava**—a variety of tropical shrubs and trees that bear a sweet fruit.

8. **habits, religious**—the uniforms of sisters, brothers, and priests that identify them as a member of a particular religious order or congregation.

9. **Hansen's disease**—a chronic, mildly contagious disease found mainly in tropical regions. It is caused by bacteria that were first identified in 1873 by a Norwegian doctor named Gerhard Henrik Armauer Hansen. Also referred to as leprosy, the disease affects a person's nerves, skin, bones, and internal organs. Today, Hansen's disease can be treated and even cured.

10. **hermit**—a person who lives alone so that he or she can grow closer to God through prayer, silence, and sacrifice. A hermit's home is called a hermitage.

11. **kukui tree**—the Hawaiian state tree; the edible nuts of this flowering tree are often used for making leis and have a variety of other uses.

12. **leis**—garlands of flowers, usually worn around the neck, given in Hawaii as a sign of hospitality.

13. **leprosy** (see Hansen's disease)

14. **mission, parish**—a special parish event in which parishioners come together to grow in their faith and relationship with God. Parish missions usually feature days of special prayer, preaching, celebration of the sacraments, and instruction in the Catholic faith.

15. **missionary**—a person who, like the apostles, tells others about Jesus, often traveling to distant and unfamiliar places.

16. **novice**—a person who is in one of the beginning stages of religious life.

17. **pandanus**—a variety of flowering plant ranging in size from three feet up to sixty-five feet tall. The leaves of the pandanus are traditionally used to weave mats.

18. **penknife**—a small pocket knife used to sharpen the tips of quill pens.

19. **plumeria**—a variety of tropical shrubs and trees found in the Americas, bearing fragrant flowers in colors ranging from white to yellow to pink.

20. segregation—the act of keeping people separate from one another.

21. superior, religious (also, superior general and provincial superior)—the person who has authority in a religious community. The superior's authority is described in the rules of the religious community and in the laws of the Church. The provincial superior has authority over all the communities of his or her religious congregation within a certain country or part of the world; the superior general has authority over the entire religious congregation throughout the world.

22. Te Deum—an early Christian hymn of praise; it is often prayed or sung as part of the Liturgy of the Hours.

23. typhoid—an infectious, often fatal, disease; typhoid is caused by bacteria that are often spread through contaminated food or drink.

24. vow—an important promise freely made to God. Members of religious communities take three vows: poverty, chastity, and obedience.

Who are the Daughters of St. Paul?

We are Catholic sisters. Our mission is to be like Saint Paul and tell everyone about Jesus! There are so many ways for people to communicate with each other. We want to use all of them so everyone will know how much God loves them. We do this by printing books (you're holding one!), making radio shows, singing, helping people at our bookstores, using the Internet, and in many other ways.

Visit our website at www.pauline.org

BOOKS & MEDIA

The Daughters of St. Paul operate book and media centers at the
following addresses. Visit, call or write the one nearest you today,
or find us on the World Wide Web, www.pauline.org

CALIFORNIA
3908 Sepulveda Blvd, Culver City, CA 90230   310-397-8676
2640 Broadway Street, Redwood City, CA 94063   650-369-4230
5945 Balboa Avenue, San Diego, CA 92111   858-565-9181

FLORIDA
145 S.W. 107th Avenue, Miami, FL 33174   305-559-6715

HAWAII
1143 Bishop Street, Honolulu, HI 96813   808-521-2731
Neighbor Islands call: 866-521-2731

ILLINOIS
172 North Michigan Avenue, Chicago, IL 60601   312-346-4228

LOUISIANA
4403 Veterans Memorial Blvd, Metairie, LA 70006   504-887-7631

MASSACHUSETTS
885 Providence Hwy, Dedham, MA 02026   781-326-5385

MISSOURI
9804 Watson Road, St. Louis, MO 63126   314-965-3512

NEW JERSEY
561 U.S. Route 1, Wick Plaza, Edison, NJ 08817   732-572-1200

NEW YORK
64 West 38th Street, New York, NY 10018   212-754-1110

PENNSYLVANIA
9171-A Roosevelt Blvd, Philadelphia, PA 19114   215-676-9494

SOUTH CAROLINA
243 King Street, Charleston, SC 29401   843-577-0175

VIRGINIA
1025 King Street, Alexandria, VA 22314   703-549-3806

CANADA
3022 Dufferin Street, Toronto, ON M6B 3T5   416-781-9131

¡También somos su fuente para libros,
videos y música en español!